NFL PERFECT PASSERS

By Tim Polzer

SCHOLASTIC INC.

New York   Toronto   London   Auckland
Sydney   Mexico City   New Delhi   Hong Kong

ISBN 978-0-545-21856-6

12 11 10 9 8 7 6 5   12 13 14 15/0

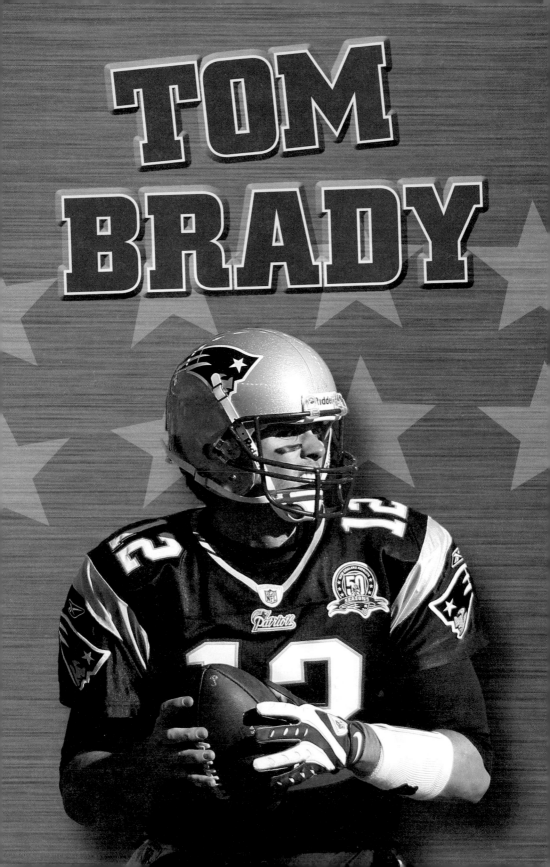

ew people knew much about Tom Brady during his rookie NFL season. Years later many believe he is one of the best quarterbacks to ever play the game.

The New England Patriots drafted Tom in the sixth round of the 2000 NFL Draft and made him a backup quarterback. Even though Tom began his professional career as a third-string QB, he still worked many hours studying the team's playbook and videos of opposing defenses. His hard work paid off in 2001 when an injury to starting quarterback Drew Bledsoe forced Tom into the action. He played very well, quarterbacking the Patriots to 14 wins in 17 games.

By the time the Patriots entered the playoffs, Tom had a reputation for playing well under pressure and not making mistakes. This helped him in Super Bowl XXXVI. With one minute and twenty-one seconds left in the game, the Patriots were tied 17-17 with the favored St. Louis Rams. Tom led his team down the field to set up the game-winning field goal by kicker Adam Vinatieri.

Tom was named the Most Valuable Player. At 24 years old, Tom was the youngest quarterback to win a Super Bowl, over a year younger than the New York Jets' Joe Namath and the San Francisco 49ers' Joe Montana. It wasn't the last time he won a Super Bowl or was voted MVP.

Tom led the Patriots to another last-minute victory in Super Bowl XXXVIII, driving the team for another game-winning field goal in the final seconds.

He completed a Super Bowl-record 32 passes against the Carolina Panthers, one more than Pro Football Hall of Fame member Jim Kelly, and was named the MVP of Super Bowl XXXVIII. Tom won his third championship in Super Bowl XXXIX and later led the

Patriots to an unbeaten regular season in 2007.

Tom enjoyed playing sports while growing up in San Mateo, California. He played football and baseball, and played catcher well enough to be drafted by the Montreal Expos in 1995.

Instead of playing professional baseball, Tom chose to play football for the University of Michigan. He won 20 of 25 games as the Wolverines' starting QB. He was also a backup quarterback to Brian Griese on the Wolverines' 1997 national championship team.

His coaches and teammates have long admired Tom's ability to read the opponents' defense, find an open receiver, and throw with accuracy. It has helped him rank as one of the NFL's best passers. Tom set the NFL record for most touchdown passes (50) and the third-most passing yards (4,806) in a season. The Patriots set an NFL season scoring record with 589 points in 16 games. He was voted the NFL's MVP in 2007 and named to the NFL's All-Decade Team in 2010. He owns the top winning percentage of any NFL quarterback, winning 76 of his first 100 games.

In 2008, Tom was faced with another challenge. He injured his knee in the first game and had to sit out the season. He worked hard to recover from his injury, returning in 2009 to help the Patriots win their seventh AFC East division championship in eight years. He passed for the second-most yards in his career (4,212) and 28 touchdowns. For his efforts, his Patriots teammates named him the winner of the Ed Block Courage Award, given to the player who shows courage and sportsmanship.

Even though Tom is now a Super Bowl hero and probably a future Pro Football Hall of Famer, he continues to work as hard as a rookie in hopes of leading the Patriots to yet another Super Bowl.

DREW BREES

rew Brees knew he wanted to be a football player when he was a little boy. As he grew up, many people did not think he was tall enough to play in college or the pros, but he has become a bigger-than-life passer in the NFL.

Drew was raised in a football family. His grandfather, Ray Akins, was one of the winningest high school football coaches in Texas history, and his uncle, Marty Akins, was an All-American quarterback for the University of Texas Longhorns.

He played football in youth leagues before breaking many

passing records and winning a state championship at Westlake High School in Austin, Texas. Most schools thought he was too small, so he accepted a scholarship to Purdue University.

After setting more records with the Boilermakers, the San Diego Chargers drafted Drew with the first pick of the second round of the 2001 NFL Draft. He struggled for several seasons but produced a breakout season, passing for more than 3,100 yards and 27 touchdowns, in 2004. He was named AFC Comeback Player of the Year.

After Drew injured his shoulder in the last game of the 2005 season, he became a free agent. He decided to accept an offer from the New Orleans Saints for many reasons, including some that had nothing to do with football.

The Saints did not have a long history of winning. They played for 21 years before their first winning season and 35 years before winning their first playoff game!

Drew visited New Orleans after the city had been greatly damaged by a hurricane. After touring the destruction and listening to the Saints' rebuilding plan, he decided that he wanted to play for the team and help the city recover.

Drew was a perfect passer for the offensive scheme of new head coach Sean Payton. He was very accurate and used a quick release. Drew passed for an NFC record 4,418 yards with 26 touchdowns, led the Saints to the NFC Championship Game, and was selected first-team All-Pro in his first season in New Orleans.

Off the field, Drew was voted co-winner of the 2006 NFL Walter Payton Man of the Year award for his work with

charities and helping New Orleans. Drew and his family rebuilt a home in New Orleans and became active in the city. His Brees Dream Foundation helps provide care and education for needy children. He also helped rebuild homes in New Orleans for Habitat for Humanity.

After completing an NFL record 440 passes in 2007, Drew produced another amazing season in 2008. He was voted NFL Offensive Player of the Year after becoming just the second quarterback in NFL history to throw for more than 5,000 yards. He led the NFL in passing yards (5,069) and completions (413), and tied for the NFL lead in touchdowns with a Saints record 34 touchdown passes.

Drew made more history in 2009, leading the Saints to the Super Bowl. He was an important part of the Saints season-opening 13-game winning streak. A dramatic 31-28 overtime win over Brett Favre and the Minnesota Vikings sent the Saints to their first Super Bowl in the team's 43-year history.

The Saints were not favored to win Super Bowl XLIV against Peyton Manning and the Indianapolis Colts, but Drew believed in his teammates and coaches. He tied a Super Bowl record with 32 completions in 39 attempts for 288 yards and two touchdowns, and rallied the Saints for their first NFL championship. He was voted the Most Valuable Player of Super Bowl XLIV for his efforts.

Five years after New Orleans was damaged by a hurricane and flooding, Drew proved that he was tall enough to win a Super Bowl, and the Saints helped the city recover.

ootball has always been a part of Peyton Manning's life. He is the son of NFL quarterback Archie Manning. Peyton and his brothers, Cooper and Eli, grew up playing football in the front yard of their New Orleans home. They would play for hours almost every day, with Peyton as QB. Years later, Peyton and Eli would become Super Bowl-winning quarterbacks.

Peyton's father was known for his ability to scramble and pass at the University of Mississippi, and later, the New Orleans Saints, Houston Oilers, and Minnesota Vikings. Archie was named the NFC's Offensive Player of the Year in 1978 and was voted to two Pro Bowls, but none of his teams ever made it to the Super Bowl.

Archie did not want Peyton to get injured or tire of playing football at a young age, so he did not let him play tackle football until he was in the seventh grade. Archie first thought Peyton could be an NFL quarterback when he watched his son play high school football. Peyton and his older brother, Cooper, helped turn around a losing program. Cooper became his younger brother's favorite receiving target, and the school qualified for the state playoffs.

Peyton's play in high school earned him many college scholarship offers. He decided to play quarterback at the University of Tennessee. He earned Academic All-American honors and set a number of NCAA, conference, and school records. He could have left the Volunteers after his junior season, but he

thought one more year of college football would make him a better NFL quarterback.

The Indianapolis Colts drafted Peyton with the first overall pick in the 1998 NFL Draft. He became the Colts' starting QB right away, passing for more than 3,700 yards and 26 touchdowns. But

Peyton was not happy that he threw 28 interceptions. He worked with his father and coaches during the offseason.

Peyton's passing improved each season. The Colts won more games, earning three playoff berths, but Peyton still worked hard to get even better. In 2004, Peyton threw 49 touchdown passes, breaking Dan Marino's longtime NFL record. His passer rating of 121.1 set a new NFL record. Still, some Colts fans thought their quarterback could not win the "Big One."

As Peyton improved, so did the Colts. In 2006, he led the Colts to Super Bowl XLI. There, Peyton showed that he could play in a big game, completing 25 of 38 attempts for 247 yards, including a 53-yard touchdown to Reggie Wayne. The Colts won 29-17, and Peyton was named the Most Valuable Player of Super Bowl XLI.

With a championship in hand, Peyton began making more NFL history. In 2007, he set the Colts' team record for touchdown passes (288), passing NFL Hall of Famer and Colts legend Johnny Unitas. He also watched his brother, Eli, quarterback the New York Giants to victory in Super Bowl XLII.

After his brother won a Super Bowl ring, Peyton wanted another one. He worked hard to get the Colts back to Super Bowl XLIV, but they fell short, losing to the New Orleans Saints.

Peyton was disappointed, but he vowed to work harder and lead the Colts to another Super Bowl while he continued to set NFL passing records.

**D**onovan McNabb entered the NFL scrambling to become a professional quarterback. More than a decade later, Donovan has become one of the NFL's best passers.

Philadelphia fans were not happy when the Philadelphia Eagles drafted Donovan with the No. 2 pick in the first round of the 1999 NFL Draft. Donovan was disappointed with the greeting, but he did not let himself get down. He wanted to change the minds of Philadelphia fans and prove that he could become a great quarterback. It will be interesting to see if Eagles fans will miss him now that he's been traded to the Redskins.

Donovan first learned to play while growing up in Chicago, Illinois. He was voted to many high school all-star teams and offered a scholarship to play at Syracuse University in New York.

Donovan started at QB for four years and also played basketball at Syracuse. Because Donovan's speed allowed him to run the ball as well as he could throw it, he set many Syracuse and Big East Conference records with 9,950 yards of passing and rushing.

The Eagles drafted Donovan because they knew he was a good quarterback and leader. He was a starter by his second season and has led the Eagles to an average of 10 wins per season, eight playoff berths, including five appearances in the NFC Championship Game, and Super Bowl XXXIX.

Early in Donovan's NFL career, he was a double-threat quarterback who could throw the ball deep or tuck it under his arm and run for a first down. As Donovan has gained experience, he runs less often, but still ranks among the NFL's best passers.

He is the Eagles' all-time leader in pass attempts, completions, yards, and touchdowns. Donovan is one of just six players in NFL history to have more than 25,000 passing yards and 3,000 rushing

yards. In 2004, he set an NFL record by completing 24 consecutive passes. He also owns one of the NFL's best winning percentages among quarterbacks.

Donovan is a great leader on and off the field. He sets a good example for his teammates, studying his playbook and watching video of upcoming opponents. He works hard to stay in shape when he's not playing and is known as a tough quarterback. He earned the respect of teammates and opponents when he completed 20 of 25 passes for 255 yards and four touchdowns while playing with a broken ankle!

Donovan also has a good sense of humor. He likes to make his teammates laugh when they are not working hard. He has appeared with his mom, Wilma, in popular Campbell's soup commercials on television. She has always been Donovan's number-one fan and has supported him playing football since he was in the seventh grade.

Donovan and his family also like to help others off the field. The Donovan McNabb Fund raises awareness of diabetes, a disease that has affected close members of his family. Every summer, he holds the Donovan McNabb Diabetes Camp for Kids, which allows boys and girls with diabetes to swim, hike, and play sports. Donovan also runs football camps to help teach youth players and provides food, clothing, scholarships, and Christmas presents to needy children.

Donovan played a big part in one of the most amazing plays in Philadelphia Eagles history. During overtime in a divisional playoff game against the Green Bay Packers in 2004, the Eagles faced fourth down needing 26 yards for a first down. Donovan took the snap, dropped back, and fired a pass to receiver Freddie Mitchell for the first down. A few plays later, the Eagles kicked a field goal to win the game and advance to the NFC Championship.

The play was proof that Donovan and his accurate arm give his team a good chance to win any game.

On April 4, 2010, a new chapter in the Donovan McNabb story began as Donovan was traded to the Washington Redskins. The Eagles wanted to go in a different direction. Rather than being upset with the only NFL team he had ever played for, Donovan looked at the trade as a new challenge. He was very excited to help the Redskins become a playoff team just as he did with the Eagles. And he was especially excited that the Redskins play the Eagles two times every year!

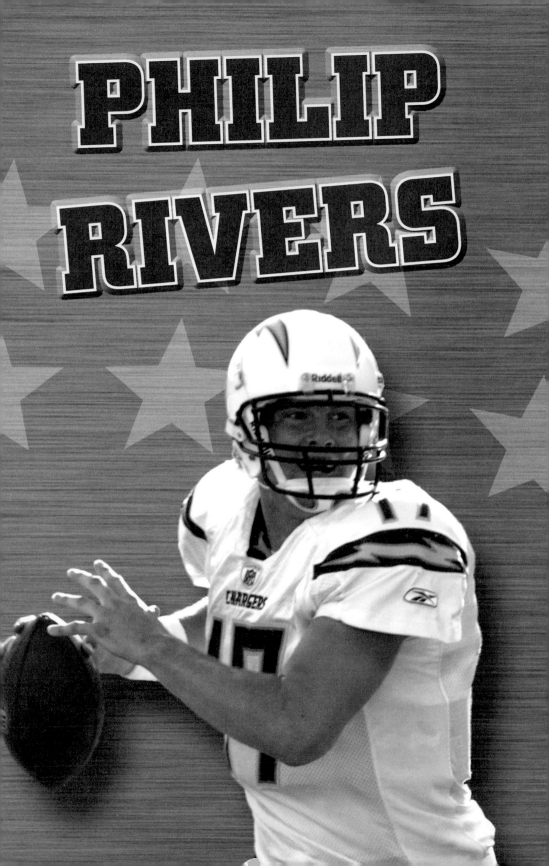

**P**hilip Rivers has wanted to be an NFL quarterback since he was a young boy.

His father was the head coach of the Decatur High School football team in Decatur, Alabama, and his mother was a school teacher. They took him to many high school games. Philip was also the team's water boy. He spent time watching his father's practices and games. Those hours helped him learn and love the game.

His father helped him dream of playing in the NFL. When Philip was a fifth-grader, his teacher assigned him a project: to make a poster about his dreams and his future. He pasted his face over the face of a Minnesota Vikings player on a magazine cover. He wanted to be an NFL player very badly.

As Philip grew older, he played for his father at Athens High School in Athens, Alabama. Philip made the varsity team as a sophomore, but his father started a senior at QB. Philip started at linebacker. He became the Golden Eagles' starting quarterback as a junior.

His passing ability and leadership caught the eye of college scouts who offered him scholarships. Philip chose to play at North Carolina State University, where he set new school and Atlantic Coast Conference passing records and led the Wolfpack to four postseason bowl games. He was named Most Valuable Player in all four bowl games. As a senior, Philip passed for 4,491 yards and 34 touchdowns.

Pro scouts liked Philip's strong arm, his size, and leadership qualities at North Carolina State. He attracted more attention when he won the Most Valuable Player award at the 2004 Senior Bowl, playing well against the best college seniors.

As the 2004 NFL Draft drew near, Philip was expected to be picked high and he was not disappointed. Philip was drafted fourth overall by the New York Giants, who soon traded him to the San Diego Chargers for the rights to another QB, Eli Manning.

It was unusual for a quarterback to be traded on draft day, but Philip was excited, even though he would begin his San Diego Chargers career playing behind veteran quarterback Drew Brees.

Remembering the lessons of his father and mother, Philip practiced and studied hard. He quickly showed the Chargers that he could some day be their starting QB.

Philip's chance came when the Chargers allowed Drew Brees to leave in free agency. Philip was named the starter in 2006 and played well right away, leading the Chargers to a 14-2 record.

The following year, Philip helped the Chargers to 11 wins and their first playoff win in 13 seasons. The Chargers kept winning all the way to the AFC Championship Game. Winning isn't new to Philip. Ever since he was a junior in high school, he has never had a losing season.

Philip is still early in his pro career, but his career passing rating and winning percentage rank high among all-time NFL quarterbacks. He has already earned a reputation for rallying the Chargers with fourth-quarter comebacks. Even when the Chargers find themselves trailing in the fourth quarter, they believe Philip can lead them to a come-from-behind victory.

Philip's hometown and high school haven't forgotten his high school days. They are proud of his NFL accomplishments. Athens High School honored Philip by naming one of the campus streets Philip Rivers Drive.

Philip hasn't forgotten his high school or the man who introduced him to football. He has worn number 17 since high school in honor of his father, who wore the same number in high school.

he start of Aaron Rodgers' NFL career was not easy. It took him much longer than expected to be a starting quarterback, but he successfully followed a legend in Green Bay.

Aaron was drafted by the Green Bay Packers in 2005 with plans to replace longtime hero Brett Favre. The Packers expected Brett to retire after that season, ending an amazing NFL career that included a Super Bowl championship, as well as many passing records and come-from-behind wins.

Aaron went to work, studying the Packers' offensive playbook and learning from Brett. He spent the 2005 season as the team's backup quarterback and did not play many snaps. The Packers finished a disappointing 4-12 with Brett at QB. Most fans thought that Brett would retire, but he decided to return in 2006.

When Brett suffered a rare injury in 2006, Aaron filled in but was injured, too. He broke his left foot and missed the rest of the season. After playing what many thought would be his final NFL game, Brett announced that he would return for the 2007 season.

Packers fans were split on which quarterback should be their starter. Some wanted the younger, stronger Aaron. Others thought the more experienced Brett was still the better QB.

Luckily, Aaron did not let the critics get him down. He learned to play with confidence while setting school passing records at Pleasant Valley High School in Chico, California. His father, Ed, had played college football at Chico State. Aaron's play earned him a scholarship to the University of California at Berkeley where he passed for 5,469 yards in just 25 games.

Although Aaron was disappointed that he would not be the Packers' starting QB, he did not lose faith. He worked hard during the offseason to recover from his injury and be in shape for training camp. He heard rumors that he might be traded to another team, but he wanted to stay with the Packers.

Aaron was still the Packers' backup quarterback when the season started. When Brett was injured against the Dallas Cowboys on national TV, Aaron got his chance to show how good he could be. He completed 18 of 26 passes for 201 yards

and no interceptions. Aaron celebrated throwing his first NFL touchdown pass and rallied the Packers from a 17-point deficit, but the Cowboys held on to win.

Aaron's performance caused more debate over whether he should be the starting quarterback. Brett announced his retirement in 2008, finally opening the door for Aaron. The Packers had not started a new quarterback in 16 seasons, but he was ready. In fact, Brett changed his mind about retiring before the 2008 season began, but team officials said, "No." They traded Brett to the New York Jets, making Aaron their number-one QB.

The three seasons Aaron spent as the Packers' backup QB gave him a better grasp on the offense. He also learned to be a team leader, regularly hosting his teammates at his home. These good habits helped Aaron make a successful debut as a starting QB. He ranked high among NFL leaders in passing yards (4,038) and touchdowns (28).

He joined Kurt Warner as just the second quarterback in NFL history to throw for 4,000 yards in the first season as a starter. But Aaron did not rest. He worked with Packers coaches and his teammates to improve in his second season as a starter, he followed passing for 4,434 yards and 30 touchdowns.

Aaron also showed he could scramble, or run out of the pass pocket, with success. He gained more than 500 yards and scored nine rushing touchdowns in his first two seasons as a starter.

The Packers showed their confidence in Aaron by signing him to a long term contract.

Aaron had to wait a long time to become an NFL starting quarterback, but he shone when his time came.